STARK COUNTY DISTRICT LIBRARY

THE WORLD'S SMARTEST ANIMALS

CHIMPANZEES

by Ruth Owen

New York

Published in 2012 by Windmill Books, An Imprint of Rosen Publishing
29 East 21st Street, New York, NY 10010

Copyright © 2012 Ruby Tuesday Books Ltd

Adaptations to North American edition © 2012 Windmill Books, An Imprint of Rosen Publishing

All rights reserved. No part of this book may be reproduced in any form without permission in writing from the publisher, except by a reviewer.

Editor for Ruby Tuesday Books Ltd: Mark J. Sachner
U.S. Editor: Sara Antill
Designer: Emma Randall
Consultant: Dr. Sonya P. Hill, Trustee, Jane Goodall Institute UK

Cover, 8–9, 10–11, 15, 16–17, © FLPA; 1, 4–5, 6–7, 11 (top), 13, 20–21 © Shutterstock; 18–19, 28, 30 © Corbis (Royalty Free); 23 © Corbis; 25 © Press Association Images; 27 (top) © The Jane Goodall Institute; 27 (bottom) © The Jane Goodall Institute (Fernando Turmo).

Library of Congress Cataloging-in-Publication Data

Owen, Ruth, 1967–
 Chimpanzees / by Ruth Owen.
     p. cm. — (The world's smartest animals)
Includes index.
ISBN 978-1-61533-380-6 (library binding) — ISBN 978-1-61533-417-9 (pbk.) —
ISBN 978-1-61533-477-3 (6-pack)
1. Chimpanzees—Juvenile literature. I. Title.
 QL737.P96O84 2012
 599.885—dc22

2011002518

Manufactured in the United States of America

CPSIA Compliance Information: Batch #RTS1102WM: For Further Information contact Windmill Books, New York, New York at 1-866-478-0556

CONTENTS

MEET THE CHIMPS! 4

ALL ABOUT CHIMPS 6

LIFE AMONG THE CHIMPS 8

SMART TOOL USERS 10

CLEVER TOOL MAKERS 12

CHIMP TOOL KITS 14

HUNTING SKILLS 16

CHIMP SCHOOL 18

CHIMP CHAT 20

WASHOE, THE TALKING CHIMP 22

SO HOW SMART ARE CHIMPS? 24

HUMANS AND CHIMPS 26

A FUTURE WITH CHIMPS 28

GLOSSARY 30

WEB SITES 31

READ MORE, INDEX 32

MEET THE CHIMPS!

It's lunchtime. Some friends are hanging out.

Two pals give each other a hug as they meet up. A bully takes someone else's seat. Two best buddies share some food. They are the group leaders, and everyone wants to eat with them. One group member sits alone. He is not very popular. He tries to figure out ways to make the leaders like him so he can join them. This could be any day in a lunchroom, but even though these friends are acting a lot like a group of people, they are chimpanzees.

Chimps are very smart animals, and they lead complicated lives. In fact, there is only one animal on Earth that is smarter than a chimpanzee—and that is you!

CHIMP SKILLS

Chimps look similar to humans in many ways. Another way in which we are alike is that chimps form groups that include leaders and followers, friends and enemies, teammates and rivals, noisy show-offs and quiet peacemakers.

ALL ABOUT CHIMPS

Wild chimpanzees live in forests in Africa. They spend time on the ground and in the trees.

On the ground, chimps walk and run on all fours. They are called knuckle walkers because they support themselves on the knuckles of their hands. In the trees, they use their strong arms to climb and swing easily.

Chimpanzees belong to an animal group known as **primates**. This group includes many types of **prosimians**, animals such as bushbabies and lemurs. It also includes the many different types of **monkeys, apes**, and humans. The smartest primates are the great apes. Humans, chimpanzees, bonobos, orangutans, and gorillas are all known as great apes. Humans are the smartest of all the primates!

Chimps may look more like their hairy great ape cousins than they do humans, but a chimp is actually more closely related to a human than it is to a gorilla!

CHIMP SKILLS

Strong, long arms

Short legs

Tough knuckles for walking

PRIMATES

GREAT APES

SMALL APES

Human

Gibbon

Chimpanzee — Orangutan — Bonobo — Gorilla

MONKEYS

Baboon — Squirrel monkey — Marmoset

PROSIMIANS

Lemur

Bushbaby — Loris

7

Life Among the Chimps

Chimpanzees live in large groups known as **communities**. A chimp community may have 20 members, or more than 100!

Within a community, the chimps spend most of their time split off into small groups. Each chimp knows his or her **ranking** within the community. Chimps spend a lot of time trying to make friends and become popular so that they can improve their position and become a higher-ranking chimp.

Chimp communities even have moms and babies groups!

Each community has a leader called the **alpha male**. He leads the group with a team of male supporters. The leaders get first choice of the best food, and everyone respects them. This situation can change, though. Another member may want to become the alpha male. He will try to get support from popular group members, both male and female. If he gets enough support from the community, he will take over as leader. Suddenly, the old alpha male will become a lower-ranking chimp, and the other chimps may not want to hang out with him!

CHIMP SKILLS

The alpha male is not always the biggest chimp or best fighter. Making it to the top is about using your brain! For example, an alpha male will encourage other chimps to support him by giving them food.

SMART TOOL USERS

A lot of what we know about chimp intelligence started with the work of an English woman named Jane Goodall. In 1960, Goodall became the first person to study wild chimps up close in Africa.

Goodall was working in a place called Gombe, in Tanzania. One day she saw something amazing—a chimp using a tool! A tool is any object that helps carry out a task. The chimp was using a stick to catch **termites** to eat.

Termites are insects that build large mud nests called termite mounds. A chimp will poke a stick into a hole in a mound. When the termites climb onto the stick, the chimp pulls the stick out of the mound and quickly eats the termites.

Termite fishing stick

Termite mound

Scientists had believed only humans were smart enough to use tools. Goodall's discovery showed the world that chimps were smart enough to do this, too!

Chimps choose their termite fishing sticks very carefully. They look for sticks that are the right length and thickness. They also look for sticks that are soft enough to bend.

CHIMP SKILLS

Clever Tool Makers

Smart chimps don't just use tools, they actually make tools, too!

Chimps can't always find termite fishing sticks just lying around, so they make them. They pull leaves and small twigs off of a branch until they have made it into the perfect tool for termite fishing.

This shows scientists something very important about chimps. They are smart enough to understand what task they want to carry out and what problems they may face. They then figure out how to solve the problems by using a tool. They are able to plan ahead and make the tool they need.

Chimp Skills

Scientists have seen chimps arrive at a termite mound carrying a stick that they have prepared earlier. This shows that the chimps planned to go to the mound and, before leaving, made a tool to take with them!

A chimp making a termite fishing stick.

CHIMP TOOL KITS

Most of the tools that chimps use are for collecting or preparing food. Chimpanzees eat many different foods, including plants, nuts, honey, insects, and even small animals.

Nuts are a good food for chimps, but they are trapped inside a hard shell. That's not a problem for a chimp with a hammer and **anvil**. Chimps place a nut on a large rock, or anvil. Then they use a smaller rock as a hammer to crack open the nut. Chimps sometimes wait two or three hours for their turn to use an anvil rock that is close to a nut tree.

Honey is another favorite chimp treat. Chimps use branches as clubs to smash beehives so they can get to the honey inside.

> Chimps may not have blenders in the jungle, but they know how to make tasty juice. They squash a mixture of leaves and fruit into their mouths and then squeeze out any juice against their teeth.

Chimp Skills

Hunting Skills

Chimpanzees sometimes hunt for small animals such as monkeys, wild pigs, and antelopes.

A hunting party will mostly be made up of male chimps and may have 30 or more members.

Some chimps in the hunting party act as drivers. They drive, or push, the **prey** in a certain direction. Other chimps work as blockers. They block the prey's escape routes. Other members of the hunting party will be captors. These chimps wait in the right place to capture and kill the prey as the drivers force it toward them. It can take young chimps up to 20 years to learn how to successfully carry out their job during the hunt.

After the kill, the meat is shared. The highest-ranking hunters get the biggest share!

CHIMP SKILLS

In one community, chimps have been seen sharpening the ends of sticks with their teeth to make spears. They poke the spear into a tree hole where a small animal, such as a bushbaby, is hiding. They keep jabbing until the injured animal tries to run away. Then they capture it!

Alpha male

Prey

CHiMP SCHOOL

Chimps are born smart, but they must learn to make and use tools. They do this by watching their mothers, older friends, and relatives.

Like all apes, chimps normally give birth to one baby at a time. The mother carries the baby on her belly and back for its first two years. She feeds it milk from her body until it is about four. This means the baby has lots of time to learn important skills. It watches its mother find food and use tools to fish for termites or crack nuts. Eventually, the young chimp tries using tools itself.

Two young chimps try to figure out how to catch termites.

Smart chimp mothers teach their babies tool skills, too. Scientists have seen a mother show her baby the best way to hold a hammer stone. Another mother showed her baby how to move a nut on a rock anvil into a better position for cracking!

Young chimps stick close to their mothers.

Chimps can be very caring animals. If a mother chimp dies, her baby might be adopted by a relative, such as an older sister, or by an unrelated chimp. In one chimp family a baby was raised by its grandmother after its mother died.

CHIMP SKILLS

CHIMP CHAT

With friends to be made, fights to be fought, food to be found, and games to be played, chimps always have plenty to say.

Chimps **communicate**, or "talk," by making faces, moving their bodies, and using sounds, such as panting noises, hoots, and screams. They also mix up sounds, facial expressions, and movements in different ways to give different meanings.

One very important chimp activity is grooming. A chimp will carefully look through another chimp's fur, picking out dirt, scabs, or ticks. Grooming keeps the fur clean, but it is also an important way for chimps to interact with each other. Supporters groom their leader. Friends groom each other to strengthen their bond. A chimp may even groom a rival to calm him and avoid a fight.

This face means "I'm afraid!"

CHIMP SKILLS

Just like humans, chimps use touch to communicate. They kiss, tickle, touch hands, and pat each other on the back. A chimp will also give an unhappy friend a big hug to cheer him or her up!

A chimp grooms his friend.

Washoe, the Talking Chimp

As scientists began to understand more about chimp intelligence, some scientists wanted to know if a chimp could ever talk with a human.

American scientists Beatrix and Allen Gardner knew that chimps used their hands to communicate. They decided to teach a chimp **American Sign Language**, the sign language used by deaf people.

In 1966, the Gardners began work with a baby chimp named Washoe. Washoe loved to be tickled, so she was taught the sign for "more." Washoe soon learned that "more" could be used in other ways and learned to sign for "more food" and "more drink." Washoe even learned to combine signs, such as "open food drink" to describe the Gardners' refrigerator!

Washoe learned around 250 words in her lifetime. She was the first non-human in history to talk to humans using their own language.

Washoe lived with other chimps and adopted a baby chimp named Loulis. Washoe taught Loulis to use sign language without any help from humans. She even invented a sign for Loulis, an "L" signed at the end of the nose without movement.

Washoe the chimpanzee in 1995

SO HOW SMART ARE CHIMPS?

Scientists who work with chimps say they learn fast and have good memories.

In Japan, a group of chimps was taught the numbers 1 through 9. The chimps were then shown the numbers mixed up on a computer screen. As soon as a chimp touched the number 1, the other numbers turned to blank squares. The chimp then had to remember the positions of the numbers on the screen and press them in the correct order.

Amazingly, even when the numbers were on the screen for less than a second, the chimps could still complete the task correctly 8 out of 10 times. Human university students only got the task right 4 times out of 10!

CHIMP SKILLS

If a chimp watches a person put a coin into a slot machine, open the drawer, and take out a packet of raisins, it will immediately carry out the task when it is given a coin.

A chimp tries the memory test.

First the mixed up numbers flash up on the screen.

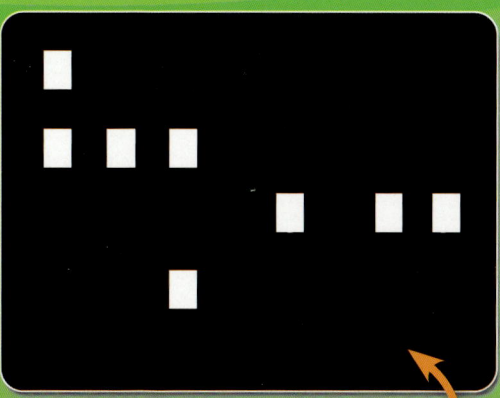

Then the numbers turn to blank squares.

HUMANS AND CHIMPS

Humans have not always been kind or respectful in their treatment of chimps.

In the 1800s, European hunters visited Africa's forests to shoot chimps as hunting trophies. Some baby chimps were brought back to live in Europe. The little chimps were often dressed in human clothes and made to copy human actions. They were treated as humanlike, hairy clowns. Soon chimps were performing on stage, in circuses, and later in movies and TV shows. Many chimps were forced to live unhappy lives in zoos. They were kept in small, empty cages with no other chimps for company.

When scientists discovered how closely related humans and chimps are, some of them began to use chimpanzees in experiments to find cures for human diseases. Chimps were brought from Africa to live in laboratories, often alone in empty cages. The U.S. Air Force even used chimps to test how space travel might affect the human body. Many chimps were seriously injured and killed during these terrifying tests.

Today, **animal welfare groups** have been successful at stopping medical experiments on chimps in many countries. Many people also speak out against making chimps perform for human entertainment.

CHIMP SKILLS

The story of Gregoire the chimpanzee shows how badly some humans have treated chimpanzees. In 1944, a baby chimp, named Gregoire, was taken to the Brazzaville Zoo in the Republic of Congo, in Africa. Gregoire spent over 45 years alone in a small cage. In the 1990s, the Jane Goodall Institute rescued Gregoire from this lonely life. He spent the last years of his life happy, with chimpanzee friends, at a center run by the Jane Goodall Institute.

Years of poor food and bad care at the zoo left Gregoire thin, balding, and almost toothless.

At the Jane Goodall Institute center, Gregoire enjoyed a birthday party every year!

A Future With Chimps

One hundred years ago, around one million chimps lived in the wild in Africa. Today, chimps are **endangered**, and fewer than 300,000 are left.

Large companies cut down the chimp's forest home for lumber, leaving chimps nothing to eat and nowhere to live. Chimps are also hunted illegally for food and kidnapped to be sold in the illegal pet trade. Laws protect the forests and the chimps. With thousands of dollars to be made, however, people ignore the laws. More must be done to catch and punish these people. Helping people to find other ways to earn money is important, too.

Many people in Africa cut down the forest to burn as fuel or to clear for growing food. Organizations, such as the Jane Goodall Institute, look for ways to help local people, the forest, and the chimps. One way they help is by teaching farmers how to keep their soil healthy. This means the farmers can grow crops in the same fields each year and don't need to cut down the forest to dig new fields.

We must work hard to protect our chimp cousins for the future!

CHIMP SKILLS

A mother chimp will teach and care for her baby for up to six years. This is good for baby chimps, but it means that each female will only have time to raise four to six babies in her life. This means chimpanzee numbers grow very slowly.

GLOSSARY

alpha male (AL-fuh MAYL)
The lead male in a group of animals. Alpha is the first letter of the Greek alphabet.

American Sign Language (ASL)
(uh-MER-uh-ken SYN LANG-gwij)
A type of sign language used by deaf people in North America. ASL speakers communicate using hand movements combined with facial expressions and body movements.

animal welfare groups
(A-nuh-mul WEL-fer GROOPS)
Organizations that carry out work to stop the mistreatment of animals. They might work with farm animals, pets, or animals in zoos to make sure the animals are treated with respect and have good living conditions.

anvil (AN-vul)
A heavy block, usually made of metal, that is used as a base when striking, or hammering, other objects.

ape (AYP)
A member of a group of primates that includes gibbons, chimpanzees, bonobos, orangutans, and gorillas. Apes are intelligent and have no tails, and most have large bodies.

communicate
(kuh-MYOO-nih-kayt)
To share facts or feelings.

community
(kuh-MYOO-nih-tee)
A group of living things that live

together, or the name for a large group of chimpanzees that live together.

endangered (in-DAYN-jerd)
In danger of no longer existing.

monkey (MUNG-kee)
A member of the primate group of animals, such as a spider monkey or baboon. There are over 250 different types of monkeys. Most monkeys have small bodies and long tails.

prey (PRAY)
An animal that is hunted by another animal for food.

primate (PRY-mayt)
A member of the animal group known as primates. The group includes prosimians, monkeys, apes, and humans. Primates are mammals. They are warm-blooded animals that have backbones and hair, breathe air, and feed milk to their young.

prosimian (pro-SIM-ee-in)
A member of the primate group of animals that includes lemurs, lorises, and galagos. Prosimians live in forests in Africa, Asia, and on the island of Madagascar.

ranking (RANG-king)
A position on a scale in relation to others in a group.

termite (TUR-myt)
An insect that lives in a large colony and eats wood.

For Web resources related to the subject of this book, go to: www.windmillbooks.com/weblinks and select this book's title.

READ MORE

Albee, Sarah. *Chimpanzees*. New York: Gareth Stevens Publishing, 2009.

Goodall, Jane. *The Chimpanzee Family Book*. New York: North-South Books, 1997.

Rockwood, Leigh. *Chimpanzees Are Smart!* New York: PowerKids Press, 2010.

INDEX

A
adoption, 19, 22
alpha male, 9
American Sign Language (ASL), 22
animal welfare groups, 26
anvils, 14, 19
apes, 6–7

B
babies, 8, 18–19, 26–27, 29
Brazzaville Zoo, 27

C
communication, 20–22
communities, 8–9

D
dangers to chimps, 28

E
endangered chimps, 28
experiments, 26

F
faces, 20
food, 14, 16–20, 22

G
Gardner, Allen, 22

Gardner, Beatrix, 22
Gombe, Tanzania, 10
Goodall, Jane, 10
great apes, 6–7
Gregoire, 27
grooming, 20–21
groups, 4–5, 8–9

H
hammers, 14, 19
honey, 14
humans, 6–7, 22, 26–27
hunting, 16–17, 28

I
intelligence, 5–6, 9, 11–12, 22, 24

J
Jane Goodall Institute, 27–28

K
knuckles, 6

L
Loulis, 22

M
memory, 24–25
milk, 18

monkeys, 6–7, 16
mothers, 8, 18–19, 29

P
performing chimps, 26
pet trade, 28
prey, 16–17
primates, 6–7
problem solving, 12
prosimians, 6–7

R
rankings, 8–9, 16

T
termites, 10–13, 18
tools, 10–14, 17–19
trees, 6

U
U.S. Air Force, The, 26

W
Washoe, 22

Z
zoos, 26–27